Lotus Lights 2
Designs for Coloring
34 Intricate Patterns for Multiple Uses

by Alberta Hutchinson

33. Hanging Grapes

A book list of the Hutchinson Collection
appears in the back of this book.

Lotus Lights 2--Designs for Coloring: 34 Intricate Patterns for Multiple Uses
Copyright © 2018 by Alberta L. Hutchinson

ISBN: 978-1724338327

Series:

Published by:

An Imprint of

Illume Writers & Artists
PO Box 86, Gilbertsville, NY 13776

Design titles by Nona Slaughter and Amy Joseph

Printed in the United States of America

1. Sweet Rose

 **Cut out this page to use as backing, to prevent bleed-through to subsequent pages**

2. Trumpet Lace

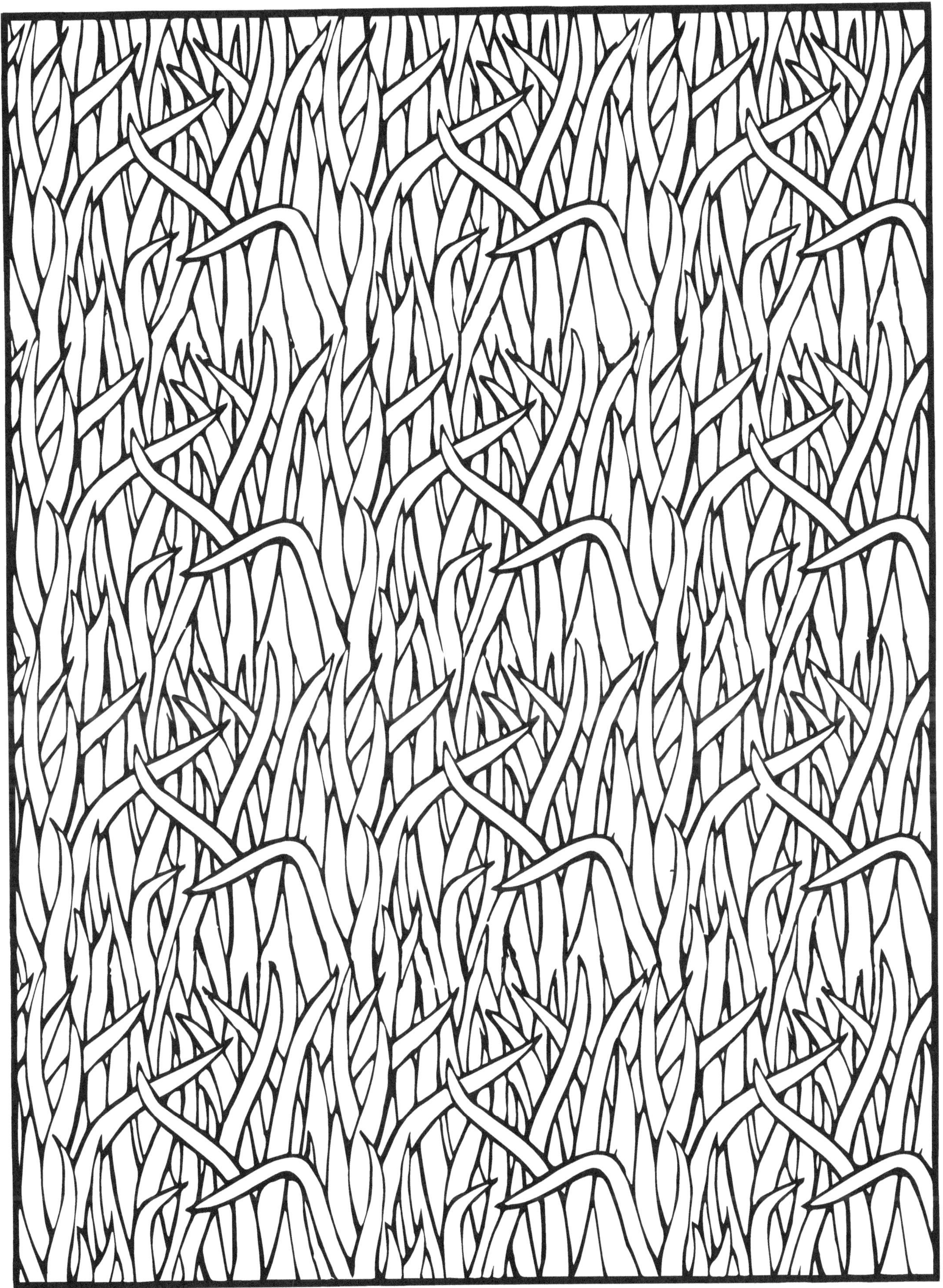

3. Grass Talk

4. Diamond Square

5. Rose Heaven

6. Lacey Quaint

7. Arrow Heads

8. Fully Flowered

9. Wave Fields

10. Clover Clasps

11. Drop Weave

12. Rams' Horns

13. Curl-Ups

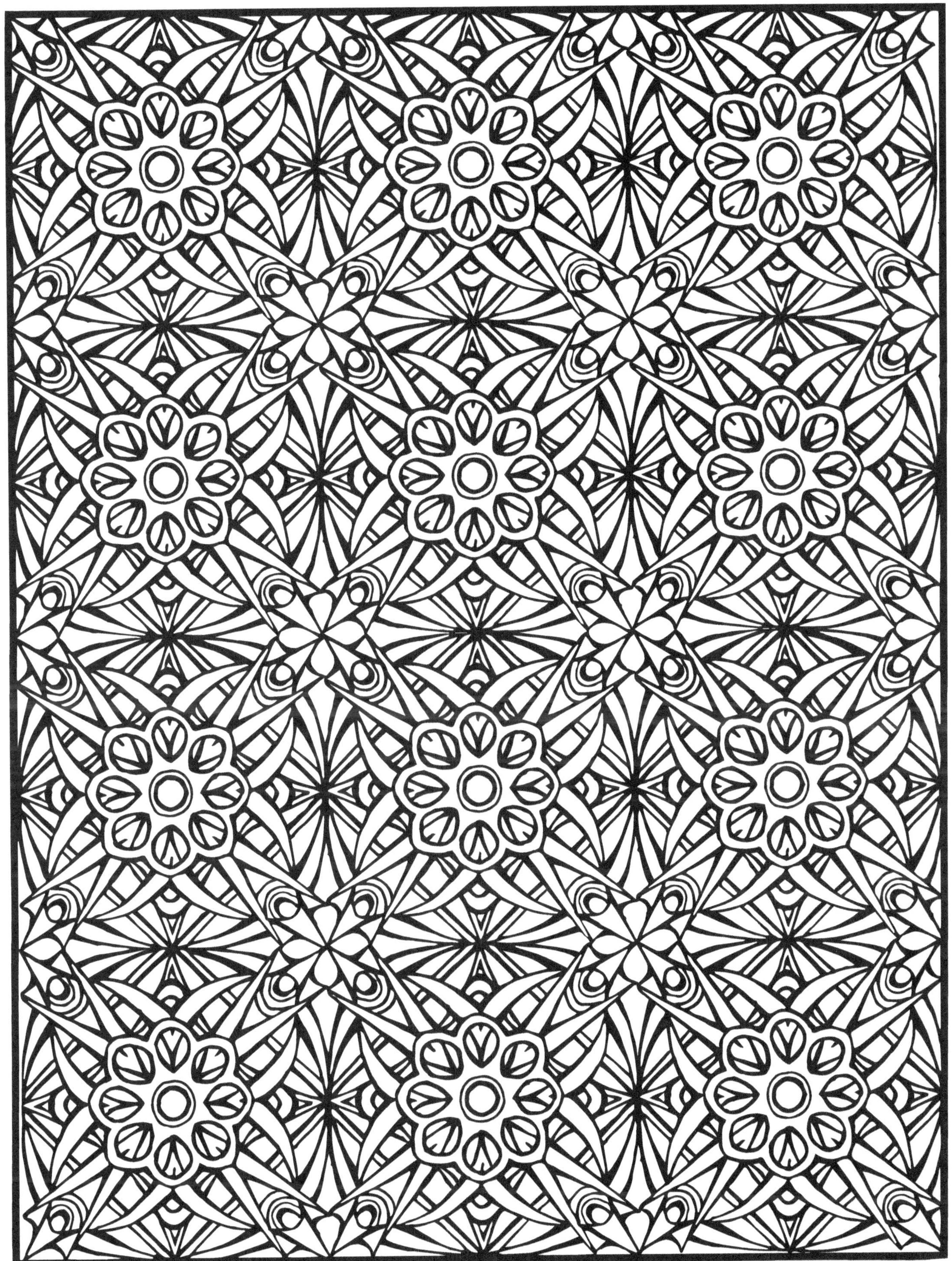

14. Pincher Points

15. Blue Bells

16. Lotus Frames

17. Sun Flowers

19. Water Flowers

20. Flowing Flower

21. Petalled Spools

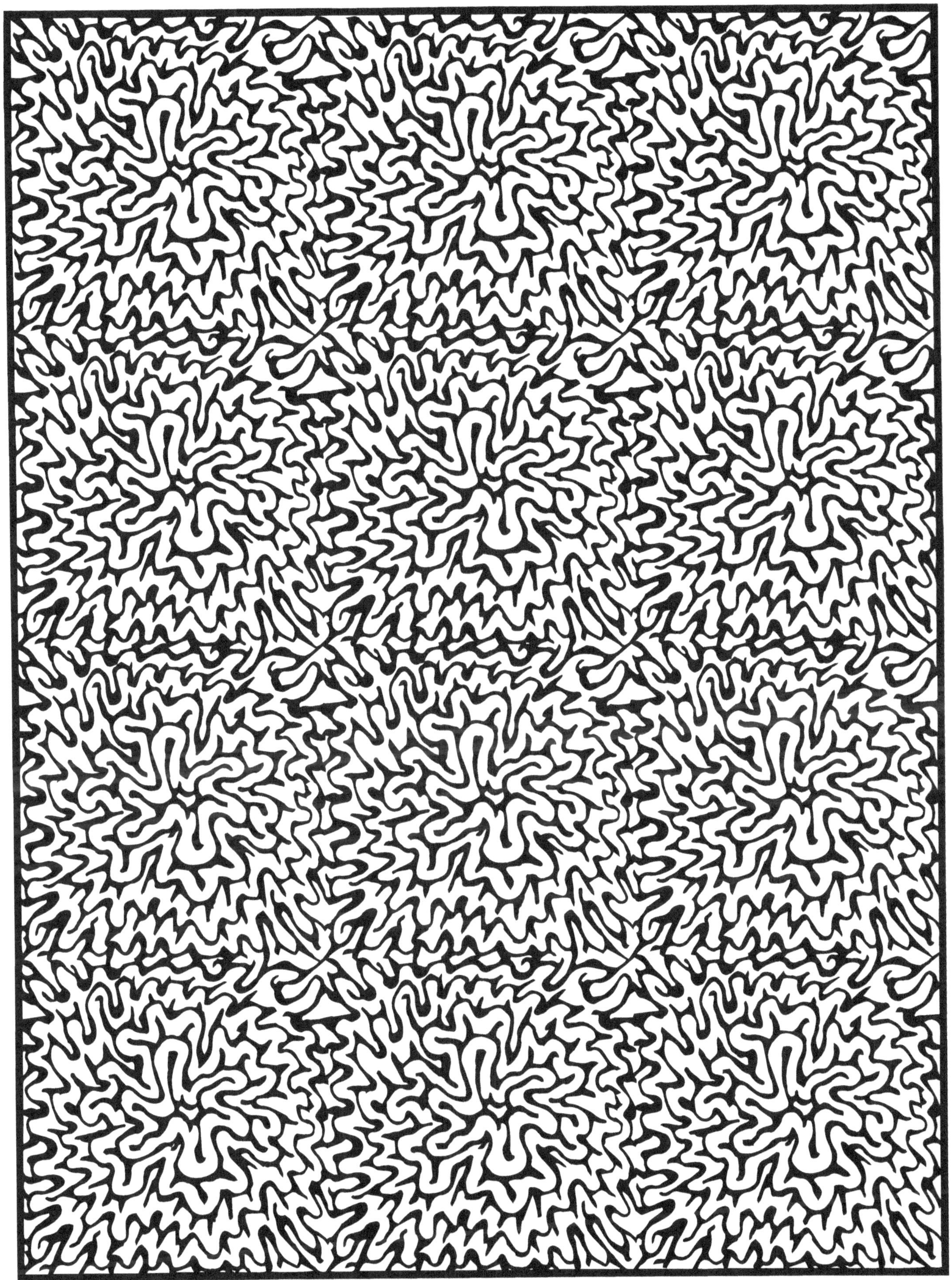

22. Splatter Pattern

23. Floral Fantasy

24. Aztec Hold

25. Butterfly Birth

27. Wheel-In-Wheel

28. Branching Out

29. Jump Spring

30. Spring Flower

31. Pretty Lace

32. Frog Harbor

33. Hanging Grapes

34. Off Shoots

Available from www.createspace.com (see specific web addresses below) and major booksellers:

MANDALA COLORING BOOK COLLECTION:

Glorious Mandalas Coloring Book — 24 Advanced and Intricate IMAGE Mandala Designs,
www.createspace.com/7242722

Mandalas Coloring Book No. 10 — 40 New Intricate Round Mandala Designs,
www.createspace.com/7242690

Mandalas Coloring Book No. 9 — 32 New Intricate Round Mandala Designs,
www.createspace.com/5479893

Mandalas Coloring Book No. 8 — 32 Intricate Round Mandala Designs, www.createspace.com/5479893

Mandalas Coloring Book No. 7 — 32 New Unframed Round Mandala Designs,
www.createspace.com/5385765

Mandalas Coloring Book No. 6 — 32 New Unframed Round Mandala Designs,
www.createspace.com/5365617

Mandalas Coloring Book No. 5 — 32 New Mandala Designs, www.createspace.com/5298076

Mandalas Coloring Book No. 4 — 32 New Unframed Round Mandala Designs,
www.createspace.com/5254882

Mandala Designs Coloring Book No. 3 — 32 New Mandala Designs, (Revised in New Format)
www.createspace.com/4614672

Mandala Designs Coloring Book No. 2 — 32 New Mandala Designs, (Revised in New Format)
www.createspace.com/4555976

Mandala Designs Coloring Book No. 1 — 35 New Mandala Designs, (Revised in New Format)
www.createspace.com/4506373

MORE HUTCHINSON DESIGN, COLORING AND CRAFT BOOKS:

Lotus Lights 1 – Designs for Coloring: 34 Intricate Patterns for Multiple Uses,
www.createspace.com/8303528

Lotus Lights 2 – Designs for Coloring: 34 Intricate Patterns for Multiple Uses,
www.createspace.com/8885543

Fantasy Flowers Coloring Book No. 3 — 32 Designs in Elaborate Oval-Rectangular Frames,
www.createspace.com/5154200

Fantasy Flowers Coloring Book No. 2 — 32 Designs in Elaborate Square Frames,
www.createspace.com/4485357

Fantasy Flowers Coloring Book No. 1 — 24 Designs in Elaborate Oval Frames,
www.createspace.com/4446137

Snowflake Designs Coloring Book — 24 Designs in Elaborate Frames, www.createspace.com/4446148

64 Christmas Ornaments Coloring Book, www.createspace.com/5186172

Make Your Own Book No. 2 — 50 Elaborate Oval Frames for Coloring, www.createspace.com/4765016

Make Your Own Book No. 1 — 50 Elaborate Round Frames for Coloring, with Text Lines,
www.createspace.com/4704942

Mantra Meditation Coloring Book, www.createspace.com/5589496

Continued on the back...

Available from www.createspace.com (see specific web addresses below) and major booksellers:

ILLUSTRATED POETRY AND MEDITATIONS:

Fireflies, by Rabindranath Tagore, illustrated by Alberta Hutchinson: 253 Tagore brief poems, each illustrated and intricately framed in full color, www.createspace.com/5074812 (all proceeds donated to the Ninash Foundation)

Fireflies, by Rabindranath Tagore, illustrated by Alberta Hutchinson: 253 Tagore brief poems, each illustrated and intricately framed in black and white, www.createspace.com/5070674 (all proceeds donated to the Ninash Foundation)

Songs of Symmetry, poetic meditations and art by Alberta Hutchinson, in full color, www.createspace.com/4019375

Doorways, 24 Doorway Designs in full color, with 13 in black & white for coloring, www.createspace.com/4389248

My Palitana (India), story and art by Alberta Hutchinson, in full color, www.createspace.com/5423470

100 Meditations on the Sacred Healing Buddha, two illustrations of Buddha, each uniquely framed and colored in 50 different ways, by Alberta Hutchinson, www.createspace.com/4938232, (all proceeds donated to Free Tibet)

Night Drawings and Meditations 2, 58 meditations, illustrated and intricately framed, by Alberta Hutchinson, in full color, www.createspace.com/6361981

Night Drawings and Meditations 1, 108 meditations, illustrated and intricately framed, by Alberta Hutchinson, in full color, www.createspace.com/6361942

CHILDREN'S BOOKS:

The Orphan and the Christmas Tree, by Edward C. Colwell, illustrated by Alberta Hutchinson, www.createspace.com/3702633

Benjie the Bullfrog, written and illustrated by Alberta Hutchinson, www.createspace.com/4734952

I Want Pisgeddi, A Coloring Book by Robert van Wormer, illustrated by Alberta Hutchinson, published by Pig Tail Alley Books, and imprint of Illume Writers & Artists; www.createspace.com/8437190

FICTION: *Step by Step,* by Alberta Hutchinson, www.createspace.com/3669073

More books by Alberta Hutchinson are published by Dover Publications, Hay House, and Skyhorse Publishing, and are available from major booksellers.